Poetically Speaking

A catalogue record of this book is available from the British Library

First Edition: July 2005

ISBN: 1-84375-144-5

To order additional copies of this book please visit:
http://www.upso.co.uk/johnfrew

Published by: UPSO Ltd
5 Stirling Road, Castleham Business Park,
St Leonards-on-Sea, East Sussex TN38 9NW United Kingdom
Tel: 01424 853349 Fax: 0870 191 3991
Email: info@upso.co.uk   Web: http://www.upso.co.uk

Poetically Speaking

by

John Frew

UPSO

CONTENTS

SPRING IN THE AIR

It doesn't take much reckoning
To know we are approaching Spring,
When jackdaws get up to their tricks
Filling chimney's up with sticks.
And ducks with down upon the beak
Invade the shrubbery to seek
A secluded place in which to rest;
And with audacity, make a nest.
Came dawn one day I heard a 'quack'
And almost had a heart attack
As leaping quickly from my bed,
To part the curtains, with some dread,
Suffered even further trauma;
My pond looked like a mallards' sauna.
Why pick my little pool to pitch in
When they have the River Itchen?
Frogs too, must find it irritating
Especially when they are mating,
And think the mallards have a nerve
To treat their spawn like hors d'oeuvre.
I now protect my pond with netting
Each Spring, eliminating further fretting.
Nature must of course fulfil her need
To such a force I too concede,
With an urge to fill some plastic trays
And scatter seeds for flower displays.
Even an old codger, such as me
Responds to Spring's frivolity.

MOTORING MATTERS

We are polluting the air with emissions,
Our oceans with industrial waste,
And depleting our natural resources
It would seem with deplorable haste.

Being madly in love with our motors
We travel to work wide and far,
People who don't live near the work place
Clock up thousands of mile in the car.

Range Rovers were once known as, 'cowboys'
Who worked from the back of a horse,
And the only emissions their cow ponies made
Were entirely harmless of course.

Range Rovers today are a different breed,
Off roaders and 4.W.D's,
An icon in cities and suburbs and towns
And considered to be 'The bee's knees'.

I may be driving along, perhaps singing a song,
When in my rear mirror I'll see
One tracking my back, and invariably black,
With its bull bars menacing me.

Sometimes it gets worse, I might utter a curse;
Which I hope the Lord doesn't hear,
'Cause my tormentor I see is now tailgating me
And with a mobile glued to his ear.

Now if I was driving a James Bond car
I could select the appropriate panel,
And squirt jets of oil on his windscreen
Before jamming his Nokia channel.

I am sure that it's best to get gripes off one's chest,
Irritations do occur now and then,
Think not ill of me, for it's patent to see,
I'm just one of those, 'Grumpy Old Men'.

So I'll just motor along, maybe singing a song,
I really don't need an off roader,
I get high MPG and low emissions you see
In my unique and reliable Skoda.

John Frew

SHEEP

I saw a flock, three hundred head
By their shepherd being led,
Whose collie dogs at rear and flanks
Ensured no rebels broke the ranks

Their bleating voices everywhere
Filled the Valley's Autumn air,
A time when every clamouring ewe
Sensed they were bound for pastures new.

No time to graze or ruminate
They squeeze on through the open gate,
To pour across the spartan grass
Like sand grains in an hourglass

Then over some stubble and down the lane
In an elongated train,
Through the village and past my gate
And cottages roofed with thatch and slate.

Hooves, sounding as the driven rain
Pattering on a wind pane,
The flock will not return until
Next spring, for lambing on the hill.

BILLY PAGE

It rained when I met Billy Page,
He owned no proper mac'
And the ground-sheet round his shoulders
Was wet and glistening black.

A drooped moustache and silvered hair
Contrasted his attire,
Yet although he trod a cripples path
His eyes still showed their fire.

He heaved along with laboured tread
Ungainly was his gait,
His ill-set leg bent under him
As it bore his body's weight.

'Twas said, when young he fell one night
Whilst lambing far from home,
And the injury that he sustained
Was more than broken bone.

No longer was he shepherding
Of sheep he'd had enow,
So worked at Herbert Allen's farm
And milked the dairy cow.

ELSIE PAGE

Elsie was a milker
She knew a lot you know,
Such as how to milk a fractious cow
And get the milk to flow.

Eight cows an hour could Elsie milk
And that's no country tale,
I've seen the hissing streams of milk
Fill up her hooded pail.

It mattered not if teats were long
Or very short and thick
Our Elsie found them all the same
And milked them double quick.

She used to dress like people did
A hundred years ago,
Black skirt and wrinkled stockings
With lace up boots below.

Nor was she fussed about her hair
That would straggle down undone,
She'd push it up inside her cap
When milking had begun.

HARVEST

Throughout the summer we have seen
The gradual change to gold,
In the wheat and barley fields
On land that dipped and rolled.

And witnessed too great sweeps of flax
In shimmering lakes of blue,
Enlivened into rippling waves
When the summer breeze passed through.

Now, above the hum of insect wings
Comes the additional refrain,
Of Combines as they cut and thresh
The rustling ripened grain.

And gratitude extends to those
Who farm their land with pride,
Whose skills, and knowledge of the soil
Protects the countryside.

Then once again across the Shires
In prayers and hymns of praise,
We'll thank God for the harvest won
And the crops He helped them raise.

PROGRESS

There were some fields I used to know
Rich was the wildlife there,
Where many a rabbit's scut was seen
And many a mad March hare.

Abundant were the butterflies
That frequented the dale,
And sometimes it would make my day
To see a swallowtail.

The skylarks filled the air with song
Rising in exultation,
As if praising God above
In joyful veneration.

Now silenced are their trilling notes
Aloft in summer blue,
In their last roundelay they sang
Adieu to you, adieu.

Today a different sound is heard
Gone is their jubilation
Their habitat entombed below
A sprawling conurbation.

THAT LONG HOT SUMMER

"There is no grass", the farmers say
"And this protracted drought
Has shrivelled up our grazing land
And our cattle go without.

The milk yields are diminished
Without a flush of summer grass,
The herds stand disconsolently
In meadows brown and sparse".

What happened to that policy
That 'insurance', one might say,
When there always was a rick or two
Of last year's meadow hay?

"We no longer have the man-power,
Much too intensive", they reply,
"Besides non have the nous to build,
Then thatch to keep it dry".

Where went the men who had the ken
And pride in such a skill?
They lie asleep in the ground so deep,
In the churchyard on the hill.

John Frew

THE GENTLE GIANTS

We miss the Clydesdale and the Shire,
Where are they now? You might enquire.
Consigned alas to an age bygone
With Suffolk Punch and Percheron.

Bred to work upon the farms
Some were no strangers under arms,
One of their more unpleasant chores
Was helping man to fight his wars.

This heavy horse this faithful friend
Gave us his horse power to the end,
His harnessed might through collar went
To draw farm wagon and implement.

A form of speech forgotten now
Like hake, and quadrant of the Plough,
Were words that left the lips with ease
Linked up with chains and whipple trees.

For hoeing, ploughing, and harrowing
Horse power used to be the thing,
Nor would 'haymaking' troubles pose
When cutting, tedding, or raking rows.

But science has moved on apace,
And because the horse has lost the race
To up the profits and the yield,
He has been withdrawn from the field.

Time was when ploughmen stamped their feet
In winters cold 'gainst rain and sleet,
Now instead of talking to his horse
The tractor speaks to him of course.

Inside a cabin warm and dry
He sees the furrows slipping by,
Tucked up just like an embryo
Whilst listening to the radio.

Some high powered tractors that you see
Have computerised technology,
So operators need to be quite bright
If they are to 'get things right'.

Regrettably I must concede
The iron horse meets the farmer's need,
I'm not saying tractors are grotesque,
But the plough horse was more picturesque.

TICHBORNE TALES

A cowman called Harry Silvester
Took the bull for an amble one day,
He was led up the hill to the Tichborne Arms
On a rope through his nose ring they say.
Their timing was good, it was opening hours
And Harry suffered a terrible thirst;
To the landlord's surprise they both went inside,
Harry insisting he got his pint first.
Man and beast are long dead, but it has to be said
Their 'photo once hanged on the wall
The landlord perhaps might unearth it sometime
Or no one will believe me at all.
A student at Sparsholt I'd previously been
But had my sights set on countries far distant,
Though sojourned awhile at Riverside Farm
In the post of farmer's assistant.

Gamekeeper Alf Millard, an irascible chap
Who at times was a trifle unpleasant,
Was empowered to remove any wild life
That he thought posed a threat to the pheasant.
I was therefore delighted one day when I sighted
A fox cub in one of his gins;
In the crook of my arm I took it back to the farm
And arrived with the broadest of grins.
Weeks later I walked to the Tichborne Arms
My tamed fox on a lead with a collar,
We passed in full view of Alf Millard's cot
Which sure made the gamekeeper holler.
But after the heat of a haymaking day
A pint slipped down a real treat,
And the fox curled up with his nose on his brush
In the corner under my seat.

HANDS

Creative hands may carve or paint
Depicting scenes from life,
And some perform near miracles
When they guide a surgeon's knife.

The roughest hands that steered a plough
Calloused, yet undefiled,
Could non the less show tenderness
And hold a little child.

Many a hand caressed a cheek
'Neath the lintel of a door,
Then waved goodbye forever
To bear the arms of war.

There are hands that clench in anger
An opinion to insist,
Whilst the open palms of peaceful men
Reveal the pacifist.

A hand held out in friendship
Or to grasp a drowning man,
Ever meets with God's approval
May we extend it when we can.

Two hands in supplication cupped
At the church communion rail
Await the bread and wine that comes
From Him who cannot fail.

Jesus offered His two hands
When they nailed Him to the tree,
To save a lost and sinful world
And He included me.

THE PROMISE

The wind blown leaves from the Chestnut trees
Skipped around on the frost bound land,
Some whirled, some twirled with their edges curled
One looked like a withered hand.

Long gone is the sheen of their summer green
Sustained from each sap filled twig,
Now the trees stand bare in the winter air
As their leaves dance a farewell jig.

Yet all will begin again next spring
Throughout woodland, copse, and hedge,
When her mantle of green steals on the scene
In accordance with God's pledge.

Then our hearts will warm to the daffodils
Whose fluted nodding heads,
Cast swathes of yellow cheerfulness
Over winter's solemn beds.

He who has fashioned all things well
Has planned with good sound reason,
And perfect is His constancy
In the timing of each season.

THE WATER KEEPER

Joe worked in waders with a hook,
To sever weed that choked his brook,
In order that a trout's bright eye
Might see the angler's proffered fly.

Some children would on summer day
Venture near the stream to play,
And dip their toes at waters edge
Midst bulrush and the common sedge.

Few folk would ever dare or dream
To trespass near his cherished stream,
The girls knew they were tempting fate
But loved to see old Joe irate.

Thus invariably before their eyes
Joe Baldwin would materialise,
They'd flee his fierce bewhiskered sight
With shrieks of terror filled delight.

His cries of wrath spurred their retreat,
No deer showed more mercurial feet,
Making the distance more the sweeter
Twixt them and Joe, the water keeper.

FLY FISHING

Who, wistfully on some winter's day
Has not allowed their thoughts to stray,
Recalling summer sights and sounds
On waters where the trout abounds?

Or sat reading by a glowing fire
Kindling up a strong desire,
Inspired when reading on a page
The exploits of some angling sage.

Where tufts of wool and silver thread
Plus hackles from Rhode Island Red,
Tied on to various styles of hook
Are featured in the fishing book.

Countless authors have been printed
Giving hints and tips unstinted,
Eliciting many votes of thanks
From beginners on the river banks.

Brown trout rise, I should mention,
To insects on the surface tension
Of the river slipping by,
Assessing food with practised eye.

Each his allotted station keeping
Some beneath a willow weeping,
Others have a different larder
Midstream where the flow is harder.

Opening up their pouting lips
Taking flies in dainty sips,
Making dimples on the river
Setting rod tops all a quiver.

Poetically Speaking

Some wrote that should the day be bright
A dark fly wouldn't look quite right,
But in the absence of the sun
The wise man would present a dun.

Yet dull or bright, Sir Gerald Clancey
Would fish all day with a Wickham's fancy,
To purists this might lack appeal
Yet Gerald always filled his creel.

To catch a trout from where he lies,
With only artificial flies,
Has been expounded by the best
From the Tamar to the river Test.

Although large fish will often lie
Well hidden from the roving eye,
Close to the bank and well protected
By bushes closely interconnected.

"The Angler's pocket Vade Mecum"
Shows how the fisherman can reach them,
By employing a method known as 'dapping'
Such crafty trout can be caught napping.

And should there be a Mayfly hatch
Tie on a pseudo fly to match,
Most fish will rise to anything
When Mayfly dance upon the wing.

Remember too, come end of day
When rod and reel are packed away,
The trout you've caught on feathered lure
Are but a glorious overture.

Because this brown and speckled fish
Provides us with a gourmet dish,
As we enjoy our Salmo Trutta
Lightly cooked in dairy butter.

RURAL RETROSPECTION

The fields I roam appear the same
As do the trees that line the lane,
Yet certain changes one can see
In this familiar scenery.

No joyous trills from skylark's throat
Alas they've gone, I sadly note,
And lapwings left for marshland tides
When foodchains died from pesticides.

Gone too the men who worked these lands
The farmer, herdsmen, general hands,
A byre stands cobwebbed in neglect
Farm buildings somewhat derelict.

Recalled too are summers when
Each cow sought its allotted pen,
And rattling streams of milk, like hail,
Struck the cowmen's hooded pail.

Beside a rutted wagon track
Lies the hoe that 'May' and 'Jack',
Pulled through the rows of Kale or Roots
Severing dock and thistle shoots.

There was pleasure too, remembering
How the Clydesdales shoes would ring,
Upon the cobbled stable floor,
Regrettably, they'll ring no more.

MY FEATHERED FRIEND

A friendly blackbird comes each day
Who chirrups when I call,
And boldly waits inside the porch
For the food he knows will fall.

I knew him as a fledgling
Before he'd mastered flight,
He showed no fear when I passed near
And he eyed me clear and bright.

I threw him raisins from afar
Until eventually he,
Decided to come closer
And put his trust in me.

His parents warned him, as they do,
That I might have a plan,
And 'fink finked' to him from a tree
To have no faith in man.

Today he flies with confidence
On sure and certain wings,
And pleased I'll be if he sits near me
Next summer when he sings.

THE BRUSSELS BUREAUCRAT

There is a Brussels bureaucrat
Who loathes the dog but loves the cat.
It seems: because the bulldog comes from Britain
Our breeding rules must be rewritten.

He says, "Your bulldog looks a freak,
We think his nose requires a tweak
To lengthen it would be more fair
So giving him some extra air".

Are they to terminate his existence
Like our shilling and the sixpence,
Who is this high paid nosey poke
Is this some Common Market joke?

If not, then I would add in haste
The chap is lacking in good taste;
Before this law gets out of bounds
Let him consider other hounds.

Now the Pekinese is oriental,
(Though by and large that's incidental)
But take a peek at him and see
His flattened physiognomy.

Poetically Speaking

So is our bulldog any worse
Because his nose went in reverse?
I mean to say, well goodness gracious
The boxer dog looks more pugnacious!

Consider too the snuffling pug,
Some think he has an ugly mug,
In fact, to be quite realistic
The pooch looks fiercely pugilistic.

The system's getting out of hand
How much more nonsense must we stand?
Why, to abolish Britain's bulldog mascot
Would be like racing, without Ascot!

What an awful waste of time
Is there a plan more asinine?
Perhaps the fellow should enlist
The help of a psychiatrist?

FULL CIRCLE

Close on four hundred years have gone
And Good Queen Beth sleeps on,
As does her captain, Francis Drake,
Whom she relied upon
To fill her treasury with gold
From Spain's fat merchant ships,
And diligent indeed was he
With them to get to grips.

"I demand this man be punished."
Said Spain's ambassador,
But The Queen said she, would deal with him,
And showed the minister the door.
"Give me your sword you pirate."
To her captain then she spake,
And with it dubbed his shoulder
Saying "Arise, Sir Francis Drake."

No greater thorn was ever lodged
In the side of the King of Spain,
Than the presence of Sir Francis
Along the Spanish Main.
He plundered Phillip's ships at will
Of their gold and silver plate,
But one of the hardest blows he struck
Sealed the Armada's fate.

He bore down on Cadiz one day
In fifteen eighty seven,
And burned ten thousand tons of ships
Did this resourceful man from Devon.
He singed the beard of the Spaniard King
And for one whole year or more,
Prevented Spain's Armada
From attacking England's shore.

How would Drake respond today
To the growing Spanish Fleet,
That plunders England's fishing grounds
Causing fish stocks to deplete?
They take our Cod and Herring
The silver bounty of our seas
While the Fishermen of England
Watch the sword of Damocles.

Do not our country's trawlermen
Feel the Spaniards at their throats?
Our skippers cannot pay their way
And some have burned their boats.
So, with history turned full circle
What other comment can I make,
Except hope our land will raise a man
As resolute as Drake.

YACHTING MEMORIES

Broad reaching down the Swatchway
With the wind upon the beam,
Poole harbour lay behind us
And the wharf was barely seen.

When just abreast of Old Harry rock
'Psalm' lifted to the swell,
We set course for the Needles
A mark we knew so well.

The wind lay just abaft the beam
Her sails were full and set,
We cantered with white horses
We'd soon be there, no sweat.

Then a wooden ketch bound t'other way
With a bone between her teeth,
Caused me to think my press of sail
Was due for a timely reef.

In half an hour the steepening sea
Was running cross trees high,
But at last we passed the lighthouse
And the sea-wife gave a sigh.

Our little sloop had done us proud
Well fitted out and sound,
At least we hadn't foundered
Been pooped, or run aground.

The maroons went up in the early hours,
And the lifeboat left the quay,
To seek a yacht dismasted
Thank God it wasn't me.

Our prayers were for the lifeboat men
And all caught under sail,
For we lay snug in harbour
And they were in the gale.

THE DISAPPEARING PUB

I went to a pub
For a beer and some grub,
Said the landlord "Good morning, nice day",
I said "Pour me a beer
I'm feeling quite queer,
And my horse needs a bundle of hay".

The heat was quite shocking,
The nag's knees were knocking
For the Inn was on top of the hill,
I thought 'They should pay me
For my effort you see,
Or else knock a large lump off my bill'.

My beer came in due course,
Plus the hay for my horse,
And mine host said, "Six pounds if you please"
I said, "You've got a sauce",
But he showed no remorse
As my legs buckled under my knees.

Then a chap at the bar
Said, "Have you come far?"
I replied, "No, not a long way
I was just riding by
And thought I might try
A pint of the brew, and some hay."

I took a sip of the beer,
It was not very clear
Rather muddy in fact you might say,
And the chap at the bar
Said, "Have you come far?"
And my horse nudged his arm and said "Neigh."

After quaffing off two
Of this lethal brown brew,
It was time to partake of some lunch,
And the chap at the bar
Said, "Have you come far?"
As I ordered a nut cutlet crunch.

I came back the next day,
The very same way,
But the pub was no longer there!
The shock was profound
There was no one around,
I collapsed in a heap of despair.

Then a voice from afar,
Said, "Ah, there you are."
Yet not a soul was in sight I could see,
Just the place near the Wood
Where the pub once had stood,
And that voice still enquiring of me.

As I despondently rode
To my modest abode,
A car drew up riddled with rust,
It was the chap from the bar
Who said, "Have you come far?"
Then drove off in a red cloud of dust.

Now I'm acutely aware,
It would be grossly unfair,
To inflict on you more of this theme,
I'm relieved just to say
When I awoke the next day,
It had been a nonsensical dream.

THE ELUSIVE MUSE

According to Greek mythology
Music, drama, and poetry,
Were rescued from a slight decline
By Zeus and Mnemosyne,
Who had nine daughters; such good news
For these young ladies formed 'The Muse',
To assist musician, dramatist and bard,
Painters and others of the avant garde;
Who sought inspiration in no small part
In each his own specific art.

But how parched and arid it can be
Sometimes when writing poetry.
Please note she is not always there,
The darling muse can be unfair.
You are aware of what you want to say
But the theme contrives to slip away,
When customary poetic fluency
Takes leave on a bout of truancy.

I have written thus dear friends because
The Ode I'd planned never was
It seems, destined to see the light of day,
So there had to be another way.
In an act of desperation
And with the muse out on vacation,
Despite the enervating August heat
I sweated on to complete
This frivolous, but factual frolic
Accompanied by a gin and tonic.

A LAMENTABLE WORD

From a poets' view, I rue the day
When a blithesome word was snatched away,
Purloined it seems as a substitute
To describe a lifestyle dissolute.

Many bards in olden times
Were aware of its value in their rhymes,
An adjective of immense worth,
Light-hearted, carefree, full of mirth.

It was a pleasant much-loved word,
Descriptive and quite often heard,
Used alike by old and young
And in love songs often sung;
One favoured by the lyricist
And light-hearted humorist,
I feel a certain desolation
That it should suffer pejoration.

Oh spritely word, regrettably
You're banned from my vocabulary.
"What is the word?" I hear you say,
The blighted word, my friends, is 'gay'.

THE DANCING DUCK

Paddy walked into a pub
And put a large tin on the bar,
Said "good morning", to the landlord
And ordered up a jar.

Then from his coat he took a duck
And stood it on the tin
Where it danced away quite merrily
In a style most genuine.

The landlord, who was most impressed
At this bar-top piece of action,
Asked Paddy if he'd sell to him
His novel new attraction.

And he replied: "Why that I will,
You're on a winner that's for sure,
The duck will pull the punters in
From here to Kerriemuir."

"Before I leave, here's my address
And the number of my 'phone,
If any problems should arise
You can call me up at home."

Late that night the landlord rang,
"Your duck's performed tip top,
He's been dancing on his tin all night
But how do I make him stop?"

Said Paddy: "That's no problem Sir
He will stop without a doubt,
Just pick him up, remove the lid,
And blow the candle out".

HOT AIR

The Montgolfier brothers from Annonay,
A little town in France,
Stumbled on a great idea
That came to them by chance.

As they were paper makers
They discovered that they could,
Fabricate a small balloon
And fuel the thing with wood.

The model was successful,
They were filled with joy and pride,
So they built a really massive one
To take them for a ride.

Up and away on the first calm day
What a sight to see,
It was November the twenty first
In seventeen eighty-three.

All science was astounded
At this inventive new creation,
Then someone conjured up a name
And called it 'Aviation'.

FLIGHT TALK

Over NAAFI tea and piece of cake
Some airman did submit,
That their part of the aircraft
Was "the more essential bit".

"Well the airframe's most important."
Claimed a rigger with great pride,
"With ailerons and rudder bar
And Control wires fixed inside."

"But that's only just a platform."
Said an armourer, with some sting,
"For concealing my eight Browning guns
In the front edge of the wing."

Then an 'erk' who fixed the instruments
Piped, "hang on just a mo',
The pilot needs a compass
To show him where to go!"

"And the whole kite's flipping useless"
Voiced a fitter with true flair,
"Without my Merlin engine
To drag it through the air."

"Right then, let's be having you!"
Said Chiefy, passing by,
"Get those panels buttoned up,
The C.O. wants to fly."

LEST WE FORGET

They came from city, town and farm
from factory, shop and stall,
With the optimism of their youth
in response to England's call.

Some joined the regiments in which
their forbears served and died,
And fought beneath their battle-flag
with a measurement of pride.

Midst the bitter smell of powder
and the sound of shot and shell,
In the carnage of the battle fronts
they acquitted themselves well.

There were men who died in a sea of mud
and men who died at sea,
Whilst others duelled in the sky above
to keep our nation free.

And countless mothers knelt and prayed
to our God who changeth not,
That in the heat of battles fierce
their sons be not forgot.

AS WE REMEMBER

Our Island history it appears
Is so much dross to some,
Who deny the freedom we enjoy
Derives from battles won.

Though faceless men take up the pen
To rewrite history,
We who remain and know the truth
Will guard it steadfastly.

Remembered are those desperate years
Of conflict, and the scenes
Where men in mortal combat
Gave their lives, their hopes and dreams.

"They were lions led by donkeys",
Someone forthrightly said,
Does political correctness now
Seek to betray our dead?

Pray, as we honour those who fought
And comrades who were slain,
That the blood the flower of Britain shed
Has not been shed in vain.

POSTED TO INDIA

When I was a stripling,
I read Rudyard Kipling
And was impressed by his keen observations,
One could smell the dry dust
The intrigue and the lust,
From Bombay to the lush hill plantations.

When the war came along
I volunteered with the throng,
And donned the Royal Air Force blue,
Completed my training
Without much complaining,
Before joining an overseas queue.

To my great surprise,
Right in front of my eyes,
Believe it or not if you will,
I was destined for a town
In the jewel in the crown
As I collected my new khaki drill.

We left Liverpool,
It was winter and cool,
And the seas were a mountainous grey,
Even high on a crest
We could not see the rest
Of the Convoy, which was covered in spray.

My first glimpse of Bombay
On a sweltering day,
In my mind is indelibly etched,
Especially the palms,
Beseeching for alms
Forever towards me outstretched.

At an ungodly hour
We arrived at Peshawar,
In that rocky North West frontier State,
Where the fierce eyed pathans
Caused a lot of alarms,
And the kite hawks swiped food from ones plate.

I went flying one day,
Above the old Khyber way,
My pilot was flight sergeant Kettle,
And the plane we were in
Was of canvas and string,
A Wapiti, but in very fine fettle.

He took considerable care
To maintain lots of air,
Between us and the old Khyber trail
For it could quite well transpire
That the tribesmen might fire,
A volley of rounds at our tail.

When the monsoon was late
We were hot and irate,
It was just as the guru's predicted,
We could not take a shower
At any odd hour,
Our ablutions were severely restricted.

At the end of the drought
The whole squadron ran out,
Each man nude as the day he was born,
We stood in high hope
With our hands on our soap,
And our eyes on the forthcoming storm.

Then came the refrain
Of the sweet smelling rain,
Like stair-rods it fell from the sky,
And I think I should mention
As we stood to attention,
Not one airman batted an eye.

There were wallahs galore
To do every chore,
But the best we considered by far,
Who worked late every night
Until dawns breaking light,
Were the wallahs who brought us our char.

I have toured round Lahore
And been based at Cawnpore,
Also sojourned awhile at Lucknow,
Yet wherever I went
There was always the scent,
Of spiced curry, and dust, and the cow.

John Frew

ROYAL MAIL

The lonely sometimes wait for him
Hoping for a chat,
Whilst others dread the sound of mail
Dropping on their mat.

The Postman is a chap who brings
A range of different news,
Much elicits happiness
But some brings on the blues.

The U.S. has its 'Mail Man'
In Scotland it's 'Auld Postie',
To children he is 'Postman Pat',
A friend to all, well, mostly.

The gauntlet he must sometimes run
Between door and garden gate,
In case behind some laurel bush
A canine lies in wait.

I remember from my boyhood days
All the postmen humped a sack,
Now, my letters arrive in a small red van
Driven by Richard Mack.

UNION CASTLE

The Union ships and Castle boats
    Had sirens that made different notes,
But their owners one day felt benign
    And formed the Union Castle Line.
They ploughed their course across the Bay
    Of Biscay in a jovial way,
Laden with tons of Royal Mail
    And salads served with crayfish tail.
On lively decks that rolled about
    Ship's stewards bore large gins or stout,
Balanced precariously on a tray
    For seasoned passengers night and day.
Some travellers new to shipboard motion
    Would try a port and brandy potion,
Recommended for the 'mal de mer',
    Or seasickness if you prefer,
Whilst others turned from white to grey
    And disappeared below where they
Tossed on the cradle of the deep,
    Strived manfully to fall asleep.
Others wedged themselves in their heaving bunk
    Not caring if the ship were sunk.
Yet eventually there dawned the day
    They steamed out of the boisterous Bay
And entered seas of cobalt blue,
    Urged onwards by each rumbling screw.
But the best was yet to come
    As they eased their way into the tropic sun,
Always a time for celebration
    When passengers with great elation,
Sensing the ship's more sedate motion
    Emerged on deck with suntan lotion.
They marvelled at the flying fish,
    Averse to becoming a dolphin's dish

Make flights outstanding in duration
    In their bid for liberation.
Or idly watch and hope to see
    Quartering above the restless sea,
On wings that spanned ten feet across
    A giant wandering albatross.
Sometimes quite near, perhaps a whale
    Would surface that it might exhale.
Sea travel now was at its best
    They ate and drank with added zest.
But this pampered life without haste
    Laid pounds of flab around the waist,
Which came to most as no surprise,
    They realised they should exercise.
Thus for the young and energetic
    Deck tennis could be quite frenetic,
Whereas a Lady and her Lord
    Much preferred the shuffleboard.
Others ignored their weights and measures
    Adhering to the baser pleasures,
Preferring languidly to sink,
    Into a deck chair with a drink,
Choosing perhaps to take a look
    At Agatha Christie's latest book.
Slim was the hope they could get thinner
    On breakfast, lunch, then tea and dinner,
But hardened passengers would enthuse
    It was part and parcel of the cruise.
So the girth of some was not surprising
    As they plunged on with their gourmandising.
At night above the stern we'd go
    To watch the phosphorescent glow
Dart from each revolving screw,
    (The same that Archimedes knew)

King Neptune's Catherine wheel display
 That writhed and danced in green array.
But after so much time afloat
 Some travellers wished to leave the boat
For a trip ashore, however brief,
 In Madeira or, at Tenerife.
Where some would hunt for souvenirs
 Or trinkets to adorn the ears,
And necklaces and other pieces
 For Mothers, Aunts, or teenage nieces.
Others set off at a pace
 For shops that displayed Spanish lace,
And should there be sufficient time
 Sampled coffee or Madeira wine.
Dancing on board could be quite fun
 For passengers on the Capetown run,
At times the deck would tilt or rise
 Taking the dancers by surprise;
So a waltz they'd started in full control,
 Was inclined to look like 'rock and roll'
Giving tipsy dancers some excuse,
 When the sober lurched on orange juice.
It seems to me somewhat unfair
 That Royal Mail now goes by Air,
We miss the sight of Table Bay
 With her mountain's table cloth display
And find it hard to turn the page
 On yet another chapter of this age,
And wistfully recall the time
 When we travelled Union Castle Line.

WEAR AND TEAR

My synovial fluid is running low
And my joints are getting creaky,
It's amazing how old age arrives
In a manner downright sneaky.

I drag my reluctant bones each day
To the edge of my double bed,
And assemble them for launching
On the day that lies ahead.

And there they wait for the stimulus
Of a message from the brain,
To zip down through the spinal cord
Like the channel tunnel train.

And did you know that every day
We lose one hundred hairs.
Though a hundred more begin to grow
Effecting some repairs.

Alas, for me my sebaceous glands
Are sadly on the wane,
So the wispy struggling regrowth
Is hardly quite the same.

So far I've been spared the indignity
Not uncommon in later years,
Of luxuriant tufts of curly hair
Sprouting from nose and ears.

On a more serious note; I have been endowed
With a robust and glowing health,
Which even Rockefeller couldn't buy
In spite of all his wealth.

Throughout my long eventful life
I've been blessed continuously,
And sincerely thank my maker
For His generosity.

WINETASTING JARGON

What can be said about this wine?
But that it's young and needs more time
To build up body and aroma
Before deserving a Diploma.
And yet, it has a faint bouquet,
Reminiscent of a Beaujolais,
It could blend well with meat or fish
Or partner any salad dish.

Now here's a wine that tastes complete
Whose grapes were trod by countless feet
Somewhere near the Pyrenees,
A glass of this is sure to please.
A wine imbiber's pure delight,
See how it sparkles in the light.
It's body is both fresh and fruity
Somewhat like a Tutti-Frutti.

And so on to this Chardonnay
From Spain, which has a ripe bouquet,
It's hugely big and most robust
Buy a case, you really must.
Many a ghastly stressful day
Has been dismissed with a Chardonnay,
Though should your ego drop to zilch
You might prefer a Liebfraumilch.

Poetically Speaking

When it comes to choosing Sherry,
The pitfalls are not quite so many.
There's medium sweet Palo Cortado,
Or stylish, round, Amontillado,
Whilst rich Rioja Crianza
Can help a poet write a stanza.
And Ladies too become much smoochier
On Sherry from South Andalucia.

If you go on a tasting spree
You'll need a good vocabulary,
And may your tongue and epiglottis
Discern for you exactly what is
Both good to sip, and use for cooking.
Or slurping when the Chef's not looking.
If there's one that suits your throttle
Kindly bring me home a bottle.

CRIME AND GOVERNMENT

The ne'er do well can make life hell
For people who abide by the law,
Whilst those who rule just play it cool
Like so many who governed before.

"We'll sort them out", the candidates shout,
"If you vote for us the next time",
Yet if we do, there's little that's new,
Except an increase in crime.

A great variety of crimes exist
And 'steaming' is still around,
By gangs of youths on British Rail
And London's underground.

We hear the shout of the football lout
And witness the flying chair,
And that which started as rage on the road
Now follows folk going by air.

Is it not just as well misfortune fell,
On our bid for the beautiful game
To be staged over here in 2006,
Would it not just be more of the same?

Now Highwayman Brown is getting us down,
We motorists have all got the hump,
At the price we must pay for a litre today,
Every time we pull up at the pump.

I recently read, petrol stations now dread
Those drivers who leave without paying,
So on a national scale more crime will prevail,
Well it will, that goes without saying.

And if that's not enough, Robin Cook tries to bluff,
That the Euro is just the bee's knees.
But many people are wise and know it's all lies,
So it's causing a lot of unease.

This political mess creates mental stress,
But we still have our freedom of speech;
And many good men with a journalist's pen
Hold fast to the truth like a leech.

For myself, I'm inclined to keep open mind
As I traverse life's tortuous plod
And consider there's naught to be feared in this world
That surpasses the wrath of God.
(14:07:00)

MAY THERE ALWAYS BE A BLIGHTY

Noel Coward's film of us
Was called 'This Happy Breed',
Alas those halcyon days have gone
This land has gone to seed.

Of the parties that have governed us
Each had their different hue,
And each suffered from their syndrome of
'We know what's best for you'.

Politicians are most skilful
Some might even say 'adept',
At circumventing questions
That interviewers' set.

There's no one better at it
Than Michael Heseltine,
I watched him being questioned
On my television screen.

I was born and Englishman
And would prefer to stay that way,
Not be a European
In the EC kind of way.

Like many of my countrymen
I rallied to the call,
And stood my ground when Germany
Had our backs against the wall.

So did my father's generation
Way back in World War 1,
We've always had a lot of grief
From the rampages of the Hun.

Now I am not defeatist
Hope springs eternal still,
But what our government is doing
Makes me positively ill.

Everything that's British
And has served us well and true,
Is being rapidly uprooted,
It's a kind of bloodless coup.

We were not allowed to celebrate
Nelson's Trafalgar Day,
For fear it might upset the French
Some twenty miles away.

Up a creek without a paddle
Is enough to make one shiver,
But it's ten times worse for all of us
To be sold on down the river.

Occasionally we hear folk sing
Britannia Rules the Waves,
And that the people of the Sceptred Isle
Will never be made slaves.

I sincerely hope this will be so
May there always be a Blighty,
But no MP will get my vote
I shall pray to God Almighty.

(26:1:96)

A GARDENING PROBLEM

I am both gardener and poet
Though some people may not know it,
And I like to see my borders filled with flowers,
Then when summer comes along
I have a coloured scented throng,
To sit among and spend my leisure hours.

But one rule that I impose
Is that I plant them out in rows
And inspect them every morning as and when,
So woe betide the slavering slug,
And snail or some such thug
That's left it late returning to its den.

Now genetic engineers
Are inclined to raise our fears,
Because some things that they do are infra dig,
Their experiments with cloning
Surely merit our disowning,
And I'd refuse an organ transplant from a pig.

What these scientists should do
To help both me and you,
Is breed a snail that meets our gardening needs
That would munch all through the night
With preferential delight,
Exclusively on obnoxious garden weeds.

Regretfully I must say
The 'pesticide' is here to stay,
And I visit garden centres where they sell it,
Until R and D breaks through
With some control entirely new,
I must slug it out with snails armed with my pellet.

WHATEVER THE WEATHER

As the sombre Winter days recede
Our pallid faces show the need,
For brighter days and sunlit hours
And borders filled with fragrant flowers.

"Brick walls do not a prison make,
or iron bars a cage."
Where lines coined by a poet
From some forgotten age.

But our lives with isobars are bound,
Such ties we cannot sever,
We rejoice when they are far apart
Though not when close together.

Our capricious weather pattern sways
From endless rain to freezing days,
When bitter winds gust past our homes
And bites the marrow in our bones.

Think about the hard pressed farmer,
The crops he's planned and hopes to garner,
"One seed for rook and one for crow,
One to rot and one to grow."

When the season's lambing starts
The ewes will bleat and blether,
And shepherds everywhere will hope
For dry and settled weather.

Nations still bicker and plot their wars
In an age that is infernal,
But the Season's are ever timed and set
On course by God eternal.

CATS

Great Britain has four million cats
So I am told and I think that's,
Absolutely far too many.
I'd much prefer there were not any.
They tend to sit upon a fence
And regard with cold indifference
Through mystic green or yellow eye,
Anyone who passes by.
And if you pause to return the stare
Then suddenly it isn't there,
Like Lewis Carroll's Cheshire cat
One never knows quite where it's at.

Cat lovers may well get their pleasures
From their lissom feline treasures
But it is the folk next door
Who are inconvenienced evermore.
Therapeutic it might be
To stroke a puss, but I don't see
Why the beasts have any right
To foul our flower beds every night.
Now I must concede I could be smitten
Should I stroke a blue eyed kitten
But have the sense to realise that,
In time it will become a cat.
And even kittens have sharp claws
So I must be loyal to my cause.
Cats furthermore, it must be said
Irrespective of how well they're fed,
Turn into tooth and clawing monsters
Who aim to kill our garden songsters.

The cat that lives next door to me
One day had the audacity
To secrete itself within twelve feet
Of where I invite wild birds to eat.
But fortune smiled on me that day,
I was unseen, not far away,
The well-aimed clod of earth I heaved
Flushed out the assassin at great speed
In manner most undignified,
Compared with when it first arrived.
I heard the distant cat flap clang
Then close with a resounding bang.
The simple lesson it got taught
Was, 'don't use songbirds for your sport'.
I'm sure that you will all agree
The only recourse left to me
And every other wild bird friend
Is to protect them to the bitter end.
We prefer our gardens filled with song
Rather than what cats bring along.

John Frew

AN ORIENTAL TALE

Miss Ping Pong was a tennis star,
And she lived with her Aunt, Soo Lee,
Whose warehouse down in old Kowloon
Exported China tea.

A plump young doctor called one day
To see Ping's Aunt Soo Lee,
And because his charges were sky high
He was known as Big Fat Fee.

Fee fell in love with Miss Ping Pong
And Ping Pong loved him too,
But when his ardour became too strong
She was glad that she knew Kung Fu.

Fat Fee had a house high above Hong Kong
Where his gardener, Hoo Flung Dhung,
Tended all his flowers and leafy bowers
Which to the hillside clung.

In the rose scented garden of Hoo Flung Dhung
Ping slipped on a green bamboo,
Which made a mess on her white silk dress
And made Miss Ping, pong too.

Her Aunt paid a visit to an old pawnshop
That was run by Wun Tu Lo,
To buy a wedding gift for her niece Ping Pong
And she bought her a blue Ming Po.

People stopped to cheer the wedding of the year
Of the niece of Aunt Soo Lee,
And happy was the throng who went along
To her marriage to Big Fat Fee.

A THOUGHT FOR CHRISTMAS

Born of Mary, Son of God,
The true and living word,
Down through the centuries of time
Has the name of Christ been heard.

Soon Christians all around the world
Through carols will give voice,
Thanking God for Jesus
And in paeans of praise rejoice.

It's time for sending Christmas cards
To family and friends,
Renewing old acquaintances
A time to make amends.

We reflect on past occasions too
At this festive time of year,
Remembering dear ones long since gone
With affection and a tear.

As we prepare to celebrate
The birthday of our Lord,
Let's pray mankind will strive to live
In harmonious accord.

May that kindly spirit of goodwill
That Christmastide imparts,
Remain within each one of us
In the temple of our hearts.

John Frew

NIGHTMARE

I remember a recurring dream
Of quite the strangest kind,
Which surfaced periodically
From the labyrinth of my mind.

I would walk along a gravelled drive
On a warm dark velvet night,
Towards a stately mansion
Each room ablaze with light.

The sequence of events I knew
Having witnessed them before,
As I entered through the portal
Of the marbled pillared hall.

No one came forth to greet me
Or contest my presence there,
Neither man nor wife or servant came
I could wander anywhere.

I stood beneath the chandelier
The silence was intense,
And the staircase curving upwards
Was red carpeted and immense.

Relentlessly I would be drawn
To mount each crimson tread,
That brought me to the gallery
In expectation mixed with dread.

Confronting me was a studded door,
That's when the light went dim,
And the spectre of the hooded monk
Would materialise from within.

It had no face, or hands, or feet
And as it floated from the room,
With outstretched sleeves towards me
I sensed impending doom.

I must regain the staircase
And reach the gravelled drive,
Evading those two clutching sleeves
If I were to survive.

With a strangled cry I turned and fled
And prayed I would not fall,
With the spectral monk in close pursuit
Down the staircase to the hall.

It was then the lights came on again
And this to you I swear,
The object of my terror
Disappeared into the air.

This dream no longer haunts me
And it needs no second sight,
To realise dark things abhor
The scrutiny of light.

THE FESTIVE SEASON

Christmas carols, Christmas songs,
Mingling with the shopping throngs,
Bearing lists of what to get
For Mum and Dad, and Auntie Bet.

Some people are bemused at our celebration
With so much hype and decoration;
Clusters of coloured toy balloons,
The garlands around our sitting rooms.

"Don't forget some sprigs of holly,
Oh and some mistletoe would be rather jolly!"
So much to remember, what a caper,
"Have we sufficient wrapping paper?"

Purses and wallets take a beating
And yes we are guilty of overeating;
"By the way, if it isn't rude,
Why do we purchase so much food?

After all it has been said
That half the world is poorly fed."
Suddenly, Christmas day has barely gone
When the TV adverts come along.

They exhort us to give ourselves a treat
With a cut price kitchen or bedroom suite,
Adding with a fanfare blast;
"Though hurry, only while stocks last."

Even so, it is a happy and a thankful time
Shared with friends and families,
And the two way link of Christmas cards
From home and overseas.

Consider too when quiet and still,
Had God not sent His Son;
This emotive time which is 'Christmas'
Would be denied to everyone.

A LOOK BEYOND THE CHRISTMAS TREE

When we lie abed with pillowed head
'Neath the warmth of a soft duvet,
Say a prayer for the dispossessed
Who have nowhere to stay.
Millions of saints in many lands
Stand fast, their faith unshaken,
Clinging to the Living Word
That so many have forsaken.
You will find them in Nigeria
Papua New Guinea, and Vietnam;
Indonesia and the Philippines,
And distant Pakistan.

Their church is not a gothic arch
Or pillars cut from stone,
It lies within each trembling heart
That offers Christ a home.
Consider too, the Holy Land
The apple of God's eye
Where dialogue for peace is shelved
As guns and bombs let fly.
And from the rubble on the West Bank
Ishmael's descendant's plead,
That Jerusalem belongs to them,
And not to Isaac's seed.

No wonder then that Jesus wept
When he surveyed Jerusalem;
He had foreknowledge of such times
And so predicted them.
And has the Gospel not been preached
To every human ear?
Yes, my friends, throughout the world
To all who yearned to hear.
When the decorations are taken down
At the end of the celebration,
Dare we hope to see a change of heart
In the people of our nation?

MOTORWAY MADNESS

The motorists fret in their vehicles
As they sit in the three mile queue,
Of lorries and cars and juggernauts
As the ambulance edges through.

But such is fate, it arrives too late
And great is the tragedy,
Two children will miss their Mum and Dad
Around the Christmas tree.

Because up ahead a man lies dead
In a crumpled shell of steel,
And his companion lies with unseeing eyes
On the twisted steering wheel.

They lie in their car on the motorway
At the head of the three mile queue,
Of lorries and cars and the juggernauts
That the ambulance edges through.

THE QUEEN MOTHER

You have lived with us through peace and war
As when Britain stood alone,
In company with your people
In this our Island home.

You could have sought a safer shore
But such thoughts you did eschew,
And because your heart went out to us
We gave our hearts to you.

Then you became the C in C
Of WRENS, and WRAAF, and WRAAC,
And at one time joined the WI
If we cast our minds aback.

You are a 'British Institution', Ma'am;
(If I may be so bold),
And been a tireless worker too,
Much loved by young and old.

We adore your dresses, and your hats
Of matching pastel hue,
And your appearances at Ascot
When there are horses to review.

God bless your gracious Majesty
We are so glad that He,
Enabled you to run life's race
And reach your century.

(2000)

John Frew

A TRIBUTE TO THE QUEEN MOTHER

A Queen has gone to meet her King
And the mourner's footsteps fade,
Our grateful nation will recall
Her life's great cavalcade;
And the impression made on everyone
She did perchance to meet,
By treating one and all the same
Whether common, or elite.

She upheld that which was decent
And honourable in life,
Royal in her duties as a Queen,
A loyal grandma and wife.
She knew the hearts of people
Who, to see her could wait hours,
And graciously would thank a child
For a wilting bunch of flowers.

And I recall the honour
Allotted once to me,
To stand on guard at the bedroom door
Of Her Majesty.
The mountain of light, The Kohinoor,
On her coronation crown,
Could not outshine her royal smile
When she visited a town.

When the people paid their last respects
Two hundred thousand came,
To her coffin in Westminster Hall,
Their sorrow to proclaim.
Throughout her busy public life
She gave us of her best,
Who, could not say with hand on heart,
"Ma'am; may you in peace now rest."

GOD'S HUSBANDRY

An apple pip upon the ground
Needs rain to make it root,
A stem appears and then the buds
From which will come the fruit.

The earth we know cannot itself
Bring forth a crop of wheat,
The hand of man must plough and sow
Before the job's complete.

Then he must wait till rain and sun
Which sometimes can be fickle,
Have both done their appointed work
Before putting in the sickle.

A preacher sows the word of God,
Some liken it to seed,
Then leaves the Lord to water it
Where receptive minds have need.

Just as with the growth of corn
So is the work of grace,
But impatient though the sower be
The Lord decides the pace.

Whatever age His people are
Only God, and He alone,
Knows when it's time to harvest them
And take His children home.

MEMORIES

When walking down our leafy lane
Sometimes we'd pause awhile,
And I would claim a lover's kiss
Beside an oaken stile.
'I hope I'm spared' my darling sighed,
'The sound of tolling bell,
which would confirm that you had died
and I was left to dwell'.
Remembered too the years of war
When parting brought such pain,
But we vowed beneath the stars above
That true we would remain.

Through life we worked and travelled
Beneath God's guiding hand,
And together we unravelled
Any problematic strand.
God in His wisdom chose the day
When He would take her home,
I watched her colour drain away,
Now it's me who lives alone.
There was a journey I had to make
Long had I planned it so,
Even knowing how my heart would ache
I felt compelled to go...

To our special tree whose boughs of shade
Had been our trysting place,
Alas to find, with others felled
To provide more cropping space.
But the church stands fast in which we wed
One grey November day,
Exchanged our vows and cherished them
'Til death bore her away.
Ours was a first and last love
To which we both laid claim,
And the shadow of her smile lives on
Inside her photo frame.

LOVE BEREFT

The memories of so many things
Crowd the long dark hours of night
Which in my wretched loneliness
Puts peaceful sleep to flight.
No day dawns without I muse
On cherished thoughts of thee,
My soulmate through eventful years
And what you meant to me.

In the silence of the sitting room
I steal a glance to where
Beside the fireplace and the lamp
There stands your favourite chair.
The pink bowlegged buttonback
A present I recall
I gave you for your birthday
Three years ago, one Fall.

The day before you left this world
Your eyes were wide and round,
So bright and clear, as if my dear
You knew something profound.
Nor will I forget when we first met
The sparkle of your eyes,
And I thank God too I could hold your hands
In the hour of your demise.

Sometimes a question shapes my lips
And I turn towards your chair,
Half expecting as it were
To see you sitting there.
Silence and emptiness abound,
The stairs without your tread,
And no more conversations,
Over what somebody said.

Your pilgrim journey is complete,
In all you gave your best,
And one day my love I'll join you
In God's Acre, where you rest.
And thanks to Him we know full well
That though the seed has died,
Our redeemed souls will one day meet
In bodies glorified.

NEVER A DAY GOES BY

Three years have gone since she moved on,
Time passes slow for me.
And this I tell her should I go
To sit nearby the tree.

Where on the stile I'll stay awhile
In the coolness of its shade.
And meditate upon our life
As the memories pervade.

Maybe I'll tell her though I keep
Our cottage clean and bright,
It's still quite hard to come to terms
With her absence, day and night.

I thank her too for giving me
The best years of her life,
Through the silver years to the golden years
When we were man and wife.

I have told her too, when I take a walk
Via meadow, road or street
How much I miss her company,
That life seems incomplete.

How photographs taken long ago
Mean more with each tomorrow.
Viewing some through misted eyes
With joy as well as sorrow.

Though it is so she lies below,
The turf, her soul is free.
I think of her dear mortal frame
That traversed life with me.

And when I leave her resting place
I whisper my adieu:
"Never a day goes by my love,
Without I think of you."

THE CRAWLS

There stands a field in Tichborne
Measuring acres twenty three,
Around which a dying Lady crawled
In the thirteenth century.

Lady Mabella, was her name
Courageous too was she,
No gallant knight in battle showed
Greater tenacity.

Before she left this heartless world
She made one last request,
That her husband, Roger Tichborne,
In her name leave a bequest.

That at Tichborne House each Lady Day
A sum from such a Trust,
Would provide the poor folk round about
With a dole of bread, a crust.

But Sir Roger would have none of this
And forgot past chivalries,
Demanding that she crawl around
A field, on hands and knees.

The time allowed to stake her claim
To be determined by a brand
And all the while it stayed alight
She could crawl and claim more land.

The ground that she encompassed
Would each year be sown with corn,
The flour from which the bread would come
Thus was the legend born.

Too weak to walk, this doughty soul
Left her bed and on all fours,
Dragged her form over flint strewn clods
On this bitterest of chores.

Could a harder battle have been won
To capture higher ground?
Mabella made her mark that day
With no help from those around.

Then a curse she laid on the Tichborne name
And succeeding generations,
The House, she vowed would tumble down
Should they shirk dole obligations.

There is no son and heir today
To hear his children's calls,
But the House still stands close to the land
That bears the name, 'The Crawls'.

John Frew

THE RETURN

We loved the panoramic view
Of sea, and all the shipping
Plus the mood swings of the clouded sky
And your garden dry and dripping.

Some sunsets were spectacular
Towards the evening hush,
How to capture them on canvas
Would defeat some artist's brush.

From lofty perch untiringly
Our eyes were constant led,
To Hastings and St. Leonards,
Bexhill, then Beachy Head.

But the gradient from your garden gate
To 'The Ridge', at first seemed shocking,
My muscles flinched at such a climb
The ancient knees were knocking.

Then gradually my heart and limbs
So accustomed to it came,
That I fetched my papers every day
And never once went lame.

Regrettably, my 'knowledge' of
The town revealed a lack,
And more than once, idiotically,
Drove up a cul-de-sac.

We invaded Bodiam Castle,
Where I spiralled up the stairs
And hobbled through Rye's cobbled streets
To collapse on tea room chairs.

But how nice to walk down Mermaid street
Where I could reminisce,
On a boyhood holiday spent there
With Jessie, Tom, and Sis'.

I was but ten, and knew not then,
How many countries I would see,
Ere I stood again in the cobbled street
Of the Cinque port by the sea.

I remembered well the parrot kite
Dad paced in my young hands,
And the way it flew so steadily
Above the dunes of Camber sands.

Then I thought; St Mary's quarter boys,
Those guardians of the time,
Will still be striking through the years
When I've surrendered mine.

So, just to say we've enjoyed our stay,
For nothing we've been lacking,
Tomorrow we'll be on our way,
Tonight? well there's the packing.

John Frew

THE PICTURE ON THE SYRUP TIN

The sugar merchant, Abram Lyle,
Could well have pondered quite a while,
Over which trade mark would best suit him
To incorporate on his syrup tin.

Then came an answer heaven sent
When he delved in the Old Testament,
And because of a creature, strong and bold,
His logo problem had been solved.

In my resume of the tale
As time and space do not avail,
Some parts perforce I must omit,
But here is the general gist of it.

When Samson's heart began to pine
For the daughter of a Philistine,
He closed the door of his abode
And set forth on the Timnah road.

A lion chanced to cross his path
With a roaring that incurred his wrath,
Bare handed Samson slew the beast
With a strength in him that God increased.

Much later when he passed that way
He crossed to where the carcass lay,
And would no doubt have been surprised
To find it had been colonised.

For within the rib cage of the beast,
Some honeybees had stored a feast,
"From the eater came something to eat,
Out of the strong came something sweet."

Thus did all the sweetness pour
From that once strong carnivore,
And Samson headed back for home
Whilst eating from the honeycomb.

John Frew

WISE MEN LAY UP KNOWLEDGE

Lift up your heads you pilgrims
Trust in the Saviour's power,
And rest assured, He will return
Though no one knows the hour.

Keep looking for the blessed hope,
You lamps well trimmed and bright,
When He returns He will arrive
As a thief comes in the night.

Hold fast through all adversities
And do not be deceived,
Our salvation is much nearer than
The day we first believed.

God shakes the world with earthquake
Wild tempest, flood and fire,
And weakens thrones and kingdoms
If He should so desire.

Have we not witnessed awesome scenes
Of devastating force,
The elements of our Sovereign Lord
On their catastrophic course?

The fool that says: "There is no God,"
Will receive no recompense,
Whereas the wise redeemed by Him
Are endued with common sense.

For such as read God's Holy Book
See much that is concealed,
A revelation to the questing mind
That His prophets have revealed.

REDUNDANCY

I was sitting quietly on a bench
For a brief and well earned rest,
When two assistant gardeners said
That I was past my best.

As a member of the gardening scene
For nearly fifteen years,
I considered their opinion
Was an insult to my ears.

I'd done my stint in the potting shed
As well as under glass,
And what about the year I held
A display of Pampas grass?

Not to mention all the flower shows
In marquee and village hall,
And chosen twice to display a fern
At the Huntsmen's annual ball.

This year I'd hoped to triumph
At the Chelsea flower show,
Until the boss decided
I was much too old to go.

So now I am redundant
But accept it as my lot,
And consider that I've done quite well,
For a chipped old flowerpot.

IN PRAISE OF TREES

He who wrote, "I shall never see,
a poem lovely as a tree",
Worded it exactly right
there cannot be a finer sight.

Ground that lies beneath the trees,
is protected by their canopies,
Denying rainfall locomotion
to precipitate the soil's erosion.

Trees help with climate regulation,
as well as health and recreation.
In fact it's true, historically
we owe a great deal to the tree.

Casks and barrels from oaken stave,
ships of the line that ploughed the waves;
And emerging from the battle's smoke
Nelson's fleet with 'hearts of Oak'.

And Yews that in ancient England grew,
fought many battles with us too.
When long bows from the resilient tree
gave our archers victory.

Preservation talk is generally topical
embracing trees that are sub-tropical.
And botanists speak with adulation
of trees that give us medication.

Did not the Cinchona's bark provide
and keep the doctors well supplied,
With Quinine, 'gainst the Anopheles
whose bite brought humans to their knees?

Thus did this specimen ably save
millions of souls from an early grave,
How then if it saved such a multitude
can we deny our gratitude?

To witness the felling of a huge Sequoia
for some, can trigger paranoia,
As three hundred feet or more
lies stricken on the forest floor.

Says the woodland, "I've done much for thee,
wilt thou do something now for me?
Each species has a certain use
but is in danger of abuse.

Our greatest enemy is man
who drops us, chops us, when he can
It is the duty of every nation
to practise woodland conservation".

A FRIEND INDEED

My maiden aunt, Miss Doris Keating
Spent hours at night without sleeping,
She had this notion in her head
Thee was a man beneath her bed.

Several times a night, obsessed
Doris woke up feeling stressed,
And couldn't help but feel uptight
Because it happened every night.

An urge compelled her to arise
With very puffy bloodshot eyes,
To peer with overwhelming dread
Into the gloom beneath her bed.

When after weeks of broken sleep
And counting several thousand sheep,
Aunt Doris was inclined to think
Perhaps she should consult a shrink.

Poetically Speaking

A friend she hadn't seen for ages
Took her book of yellow pages,
Ran her finger down a list
And chose a good psychiatrist.

Aunt Doris had one consultation
But declined a further invitation,
On the very simple grounds
The course would cost three hundred pounds.

Then a neighbour hearing of her plight
Popped around one Monday night,
And with great panache and esprit de corps
Removed the bed legs with his saw.

Although his method was a shock
My Aunt now sleeps around the clock,
Whilst her neighbour being very able
Used the legs to make a table.

AN AFRICAN TALE

There is a place called Monze,
By a Rhodesian Railway track,
Where I went on first appointment
Almost five decades aback.

When I stepped down on the edge of town
The sun was already low,
And although I'd come several hundred miles
There were still three more to go.

Eventually, when I'd settle in,
After a week or more,
I arose one morn' to a sparkling dawn
And drove to the butcher's store.

It was owned by a man called Freddy Butts,
And I said my name was Frew,
He greeted me most affably
With his twinkling eyes of blue.

Fred oft'times slipped his false teeth out
Because they caused him pain,
Though remembering where he'd lain them
Could severely tax his brain.

Poetically Speaking

I purchased beef and kidney's
And some salted bacon too,
Plus a couple of pounds of nice lean steak
To concoct an Irish stew.

As I was taking of my leave,
Fred said, "It's my belief,
I've mislaid my set of dentures"
And I thought to myself "Hells teeth."

Just imagine if when I reached home
And unpacked my bacon rashers,
That I should see confronting me
His wandering set of gnashers!

Oh what relief when I glimpsed his teeth
And I'm sure you will agree,
They were having a bath and a great big laugh,
In his morning cup of tea!

If you think this is a far-fetched tale
Here's one that will astound,
All cuts of meat from Fred Butts beef
Were just six pence per pound!

THE REUNION

Robert, Taffy, and John M Frew
With Mary, Rhona, and Esme too,
All met on one occasion rare
At sunny Weston-Super-Mare.

Whilst members of the N.R.G.
We'd served Her Royal Majesty,
Through rugged times and jubilation
At Monze's Agricultural Station.

The hotel where we old friends stayed
Had many artefacts displayed,
In a fashion quite baronial
And aptly called 'The Old Colonial'.

On walls hung masks and assegais,
And heads of buck and glassy eyes,
Carved elephants stood on the floor
With statues east of Singapore.

The Army too was on parade
In sepia photographs arrayed,
Pith helmets and moustachioed
Heroes of the Khyber road.

We sat and sipped our lemon gin,
Midst native spear and leopard skin,
While lazy punkah's on the ceiling
Revived that old Colonial feeling.

The decades had not dimmed the mind
Of characters of every kind,
Like, Mwenda, Bwalya, Dawoodjee,
Or Couvaras from Chisekesi.

And how could anyone forget
Lee Savory, Allies, and Burdett?
Whose endless talk and sacred joys
Were rainfall, mealies, and their 'Boys'.

We all agreed 'twas good to cast
Our thoughts back on a time now past,
And how we made our contribution
To a solid British Institution.

We had reminisced our halcyon days,
Now came the parting of the ways
Thus we ambassadors all arose,
The Leek, the Thistle, and the Rose.

Had we not loyally served the Crown?
Then watched the Empire dying down?
We drove off feeling quite euphoric
Our gathering was a touch historic.

John Frew

HIGH FINANCE

So, the pound is up against the mark
But down against the dollar,
The mechanics of the City
Are quite difficult to follow.

In all my life, quite honestly,
So far as I could see
Whether up or down, or in or out
It made no difference to me.

When the City's feeling nervous
And suffering hypertension,
It's probably just as well for me
It's beyond my comprehension.

A Bear, I'm told sells stocks and shares
Lest the value of them dives,
Then when they do, he buys them back
Before their price begins to rise.

The Bull however buys some shares
Expecting them to rocket,
Should they comply, he sells them on
And the gain goes in his pocket.

Now, some of you may comprehend
And need only telling once,
But to be quite frank, where I'm concerned
I'm a superb, financial dunce.

The City's not for one like me,
I just haven't got the bent,
So I put it in the Woolwich,
At three point five per cent.

WRITING POETRY

To write like 'The Bard'
Is tremendously hard,
I never will match the immortal,
But I've done my best
With commendable zest,
And trust I can make you all chortle.

I get a funny sensation
And am filled with elation,
When an idea comes into my head,
I could be walking along
Amidst Winchester's throng,
Or I could be reclining in bed.

But I never can tell
If all will go well,
Or what subject is under my hat,
It could turn out sublime
From the very first line,
But a poem can also fall flat.

So I thought, "Now there's a thing,
I'll give Richard a ring,"
B.T. says; "It's good to talk",
This verse seems alright
I'll be up half the night,
When I've taken the dog for a walk.

FOOTNOTE:
BBC Solent presenter Richard Williams invited listening poets to compose a few verses describing how they got ideas and inspiration for writing poetry, and to read them to him that evening over the 'phone. This was my offering after twenty minutes work. Wed. Sept. 17. 1997.

John Frew

NEWSPEAK

Correct pronunciation should be an obligation,
Especially for presenters of the news;
So of their privileged vocation in speaking to the nation
May I offer you my comments and my views?

Not having worn the Eton collar I do not profess to be a
    scholar,
So I trust you will not brand me as imperious;
But when they mispronounce a word and make it sound
    absurd,
I regard the aberration somewhat serious.

On the media at times should they report the latest
    crimes,
Where thieves involved had been distinctly devious,
I tend to lose all sense of calm if any bodily harm
Is said by the reporter to be 'grevious'.

There is another word I dread which is sometimes
    wrongly said,
And gives me cause to exercise my 'splenius';
Such as the news on ITN when a dolly bird just then
    reported
Some young boys had been 'Mischevious'.

While viewing tennis on the set, I had further cause to
   fret,
As Henman sought to find a spark of genius;
A commentating nerd got tangled in a word
Claiming double faults in service were not 'Henious'

English contains Germanic, plus a blend of the Hispanic,
With contributions from Latin, French and Greek;
It's deliciously expressive and the range of words
   impressive,
So we all should be more careful when we speak.

(19.08.00)

THE BOOK SHOP

I paused at Lawrence Oxley's shop
One day in Alresford town,
And noticed just in front of me
A book of great renown.
Of it the sight gave me delight
And a touch of sadness too,
It was the tome that thousands own
And others do eschew.

The shelf outside the window
Appears when weather's dry,
Displaying a miscellany
Of books to catch the eye.
The price of them, all second hand
Is one and all the same,
Some penned by famous authors
And some of lesser name.

The book I'd spied was neatly bound
Its pages edged with gold,
With a machine cut index system
For its chapters manifold.
I gladly paid the twenty pence
And ruefully observed,
'Yet one more sign of modern times
Is God's devalued Word'.

AMERICAN INFLUENCE

The latest crass trend,
Drives me right round the bend,
So I'm looking for wherefores and whys.
The whole of society with some impropriety
Insists on calling us 'Guys'.

When I was a lad,
I was told by my Dad,
A boy grew from a youth to a man,
But this 'Guy' is absurd,
A deplorable word,
I avoid it whenever I can.

If one got in a flap
There was often a chap,
Who would stop and lend one a hand,
But now they imply you should wait for some guy,
On this matter I must make my stand.

To most Scottish folk a man was a bloke,
And we acknowledge that title down here,
And I've often felt mellow
To be called 'a nice fellow'
But a Guy! That would give me no cheer.

A guy is you see, a straw effigy,
Of a villain who once copped his lot,
He displayed untold malice
Against Westminster Palace,
In that dastardly gunpowder plot.

So I'm using my gumption
And make the assumption,
It all stems from the play 'Guys and Dolls',
Would it now be correct or show disrespect,
If we called women everywhere 'Molls'?

A GARDENER'S LAMENT

I ask you all, "why is it that
We suffer from the next door cat?"
That gets the best of everything
And yet persists in wandering,
Not content with what it's got
It prowls around the neighbour's plot.

No sooner have I tilled a bed
Of soil, for flowers, some days ahead,
When stealthily there creeps a cat
To monitor what I've been at,
Perceived the ground no longer hard
And promptly leaves its calling card.

Now lion dung, I've heard some say
Will keep offending cats away,
According to one theoretician
A fairly large fresh deposition
Implies, that though you have no doggy
You do possess a massive moggy.

The curry plant, I'm also told
Deters even the extra bold,
Though cherished in the Orient
All felines loathe its pungent scent,
Yet in spite of this I was dismayed
To see one lying in its shade.

One day in utter desperation
After much earnest cogitation,
I bought a water gun unique
To squirt a jet some forty feet,
And settled down with the satisfaction
I'd embarked upon a plan of action.

Eventually, to my delight
A ginger tom cat hove in sight,
I raised the gun and squeezed the trigger
Confident I'd soak old tigger,
Sadly though I must relate,
That during the protracted wait
The water had all quietly leaked
Into the ground beneath my feet.

This Tom and Jerry situation
Was purely of my own creation,
And clearly not the best solution
For exacting retribution.
It had become a pantomime
And consumed a lot of time.

Such methods are now anachronic
Cat scaring has gone ultrasonic,
A small green box with sensor eye
Checks out every passer-by.
Dogs, birds, and fish need not be fearful
Only moggies get an earful,
Which is, when all is said and done
More effective than a water gun.

WEATHER REPORT

Silhouetted against the glowering sky
A murmur of starlings tumble by,
Striving hard to reach the lee
Of the welcoming boughs in a chestnut tree.
And every sheep has turned its tail
To bear the brunt of the rising gale.

It is always worse in the dead of night
As the teeth of the gale begin to bite,
We felt its power ten years before
When it left deep holes in the forest floor,
As mighty trees like the beech and oak
Were all laid low when the tempest spoke.

Sea wives tonight will doubtless keep
A vigil for menfolk on the deep,
Who ride the storm with the fervent hope
The slogging engines will more than cope.
When the stern descends the screws bite deep,
And when the ship corkscrews the men can't sleep.

Hurricane winds during yesterday
Struck the caravan site at Seaview Bay,
And Sussex citizens sensed a chill
As a tornado swept through Selsey Bill,
Patrick Moore was dining at the town's Tandoori
When his observatory was hit by the twister's fury.

The sharks are gathering to snatch a slice
Of storm repairs at the highest price,
Forego an estimate, get a full quotation,
Saving time and money or litigation.
Carl Tyler forecasts floods and rain
And you premiums are set to rise again.

SENSIBLE CUISINE

When cooking if I really try
I can produce a shepherds pie,
Rustle up toad in the hole,
A beef or chicken casserole.
And should time be short, can beat the clock
By whipping out my trusty wok,
And in less than fifteen minutes time
Have a hot Chinese with a glass of wine.
I have a penchant too for curry
But cook it slowly, without hurry,
And am not averse to a vindaloo;
Though it makes me sweat, my goodness, phew!
Curry munching is very pleasant
I once made curry with a small hen pheasant.
But don't pluck birds, that's tedious habit,
I skin them as one would a rabbit.
Besides, the skin of birds can fatten
Take care you must not let that happen.
Like a camel that displays a hump
We too may find we've formed a bump,
Developed in winter on rich provisions
And slumping in front of our televisions.
But don't lose hope, may I extol
The virtues of the salad bowl?
Especially when it is Spring
Coupled with spurts of gardening.
For the fuller figure it's such a blessing
But don't over indulge in the salad dressing;
Just because it's salad days
Do not go mad with the mayonnaise,
Because when you've finished your bingeing fun
You'll slither back into square one.
Ah yes, losing that bulge is as much a treat
As the re-acquaintance with one's feet!

SUMMER ATTRACTIONS

We've enjoyed Royal Ascot's sport of kings
And the racing skills of riders,
With Willie Carson on his box
Giving tips about outsiders.

And watched the ladies drift around
In their colourful display,
Of Summer frocks and frilly hats
That brightened up each day.

Chelsea too has come and gone
With a blaze of floral colour,
Where the gardening pundits had the chance
To swap opinions with each other.

Our cricket's on the up and up
Now that England has new talent,
And our Rugby team has beaten Oz
In an effort truly gallant.

But we've licked our wounds at Wimbledon
Our bete noire every year,
Where every winning Henman stroke
Draws a patriotic cheer.

The championships are over
We just can't produce a winner,
Our Tim appears, then fades away,
Success seems that much slimmer.

Contorted tennis balls that fly
From racquets highly strung,
Are missiles that test the speed and strength
Of the fearless and the young.

Loyal British fans queue up for hours
And congregate on Henman Hill;
But can we win? Can we heck,
Do you think we ever will?

John Frew

WHATEVER THE WEATHER

As the sombre Winter days recede
Our pallid faces show the need,
For brighter days and sunlit hours
And borders filled with fragrant flowers.

"Brick walls do not a prison make,
or iron bars a cage."
Where lines coined by a poet
From some forgotten age.

But our lives with isobars are bound,
Such ties we cannot sever,
We rejoice when they are far apart
Though not when close together.

Our capricious weather pattern sways
From endless rain to freezing days,
When bitter winds gust past our homes
And bites the marrow in our bones.

Think about the hard pressed farmer,
The crops he's planned and hopes to garner,
"One seed for rook and one for crow,
One to rot and one to grow."

When the season's lambing starts
The ewes will bleat and blether,
And shepherds everywhere will hope
For dry and settled weather.

Nations still bicker and plot their wars
In an age that is infernal,
But the Season's are ever timed and set
On course by God eternal.

FAREWELL TO SUMMER

The pyracantha berries hang
Red in the autumn air,
A summer contribution to
The blackbirds winter fare.

And perched upon the chimney pots
In pairs as black as jet,
Intimidating jackdaws wait
For whatever they can get.

Not so the wren that hops and flits
Wasting no time at all,
As she feeds among the ivy leaves
That cloak the churchyard wall.

But the robin I befriended
Who chivvied me for food,
Has not appeared, just as I feared,
Since the raising of his brood.

His cheerful presence will be missed,
There were none as tame as he,
But hopefully his offspring soon
Will come to visit me.

FALLEN STONES

The great wall of Jerusalem
Had crumbled, it was said,
Its wooden gates had been consumed by fire,
And a man sat down and wept
He prayed and scarcely slept,
And that man whom God had called was Nehemiah.

He travelled to Jerusalem
Bearing timber for new doors,
And to the nobles and officials did declare,
"Even stones that had been burned
Should be cleaned and then returned,
Each one would help to hasten the repair".

Their enemies looked on
Pouring scorn and taunts upon
Nehemiah and the builders of the wall,
And Sanballat and Tobiah
Breathing threats that sounded dire,
Said they'd fight, and cause confusion to them all.

At which Judah rose and spoke;
"Sanballat doesn't joke,
Half our workforce must be armed with spear and sword,"
Then construction went apace
As the stones they did replace,
And they toiled with full protection from the Lord.

This shows how God can use
Anything that He should choose,
This is in fact a restoration story,
We too may feel the fire
But He can raise up and inspire
The downcast, to be built up for His glory.

UNLESS THOSE DAYS BE SHORTENED
Math Chpt 24

The world is all but bankrupt
In morals and resources
As hedonistic man pursues
Corrupt and devious courses.

Without good counsel and strong laws
The misguided revel in their sin
Even children are robbed of their innocence
As the tide of filth floods in.

We may have acquired great knowledge
Education, and much skill
But the moral rottenness that abounds
Is the antitheses of God's will.

Mankind's rejection of God of course
Was rife in Noah's day
And so revolted was the Lord
He swept them all away.

Noah and his family were saved
Having believed in God throughout
So when God shut them in the Ark
He also shut the others out.

Yes, our world is filled with violence
Moral decadence and decay.
One wonders how much time we have
Before judgement comes our way.

With iniquity so profligate
And the love of millions growing cold
Are we witnessing a countdown
Of the signs Jesus foretold.

RIGHTEOUSNESS EXALTS A NATION

'There is none righteous, no, not one.'
King Solomon once said,
Now we ourselves have been betrayed
And into error led.
Behavioural problems plague our schools
But who can blame the child
When parents dissolve the partnership
And refuse to be reconciled?
Denied the birthright of a loving home
Some children then incline
To a socially unacceptable life
Of drugs, and vice, and crime.

There is adultery and murder too,
Violence and depravity,
Which no one in authority
Has dealt with effectually.
Our statutes once were Bible based,
Which met God's approbation,
Now liberal humanistic laws
Pervade our legislation.
Jesus said these things would happen
That faith would fall away,
The time has come for Christians
To fight the evil of the day.

Academics and statesmen all
Have in their overview,
Paralleled the first three verses
Which are written in Psalm 2.
We should reaffirm our Christian heritage
Fought for and hard won,
By the martyred saints at Smithfield
And on battlefields long gone.
God can only bless a nation
When they are repentant of their sin,
To deny Him means we must ever wait
For His healing to begin.

'THEY'

"The Sabbath you must not profane,"
Isaiah said, and made it plain
From God Almighty he had heard
To keep it holy was preferred.
"God's house should be a place of prayer
And every soul who enters there
Will find an honourable delight
And receive a blessing in His sight".
"Ah, but all that stuff is now old hat,
We don't want any more of that!
Let's change the laws", the people said,
"Our Sundays' always seem so dead.
We suffer from too much restriction
And need more fun not benediction.
Christians can still go to church
It's not our intention to besmirch
Their faith, but we just feel
For many it has no appeal.
As we work hard throughout the week
Sundays are a time to seek
Things of a relaxing sort,
Besides we want more Sunday sport.
Not just tennis, golf, and cricket,
With England on a sticky wicket,
More football too would be quite bracing
So too would watching horse racing.

Then if the weather turns out wet
We can stay at home and 'phone a bet.
Nor do we think it too anarchic
To demand that every Supermarket
Be allowed to trade on Sunday,
As most of us start work on Monday.
Ah yes! And when it comes to drinking,
We alcoholic's have been thinking,
It would be nice to drink all day
In the Continental way".
So, very slowly, gradually,
Almost surreptitiously,
The Government has given in
Pandering to every whim,
Politicians say, "We must face facts
When people spend we collect more tax
From VAT, we know, it's true
That lots more lolly will accrue."
Six days God meant mankind to labour,
The seventh one set aside to savour
A time of rest for all the nation
Essential for recuperation.
Sunday was once a Holy day,
'They', took its sanctity away.

WHERE PATHS CROSSED

One day I met a kindly man
Who stopped and asked of me,
"What would you give if you could live
For all eternity?"

I thought awhile and then replied:
"Is that not wishful thinking?"
And he rejoined: "No, not at all,"
His earnest eyes unblinking.

I laughed and said: "The thought is vain,
Why else the cemetery?
Few are the mortal lives that reach
Even a century."

But unperturbed he carried on
So I let him have his say,
About the Saviour of the world
The Life, The Truth, The Way.

How all the riches in the world
Could not repay the cost,
Of Jesus' supreme sacrifice
For me and all the lost.

What did I give that I might live
For all eternity?
I gave my contrite heart to Christ,
In true sincerity.

AND GOD SAID....

You will have no other God but me
None shall usurp my name,
Do not bow down to idols
In worshipful acclaim.

Take not the name of the Lord in vain
In this world man is but lowly,
Refrain from work on the Sabbath day
Remember, keep it holy.

Give honour to your parents both,
Cause neither of them strife,
And carry out no murder for
It is I who giveth life.

Do not commit adultery
Which brings marriage into shame,
And steal not from your fellow men
Or make a wrongful claim.

False testimony you shall not give
Against he that is your neighbour,
And covet not his house or wife
Lest you incur the Lord's disfavour.

John Frew

THE WAY WE WERE

Queen Victoria once was asked
By and Indian Potentate,
If she could say just what it was
That had made her country great.

She reached towards a table
That was standing by her side,
And as she took God's holy book
Said, "This has been our guide."

Of all the many empires
The world has ever seen,
This nation had the greatest
And our navy ruled supreme.

Thus God blessed our Island home
And its ancient crown
Until we turned our backs,
On Him and let Him down.

Can we be sure the problems
And the troubles we endure,
Are not a sign from heaven
That our nation is impure?

If future foes beset us
And we oppose them one and all,
Will our God of ages past
Help us when we call?

Lord send down your revival
Pour out the latter rain,
May the spirit of your holiness
Live in us once again.

THEN WE ARE MORE THAN CONQUERORS

Buttressed and solid stands the Church
High on the grassy mound,
The rising gradient to the door
Requires that legs be sound.

A multitude throughout the years
The same steep pathway trod,
To keep their Christian faith alive
And spend some time with God.

When we believe in Jesus
And repent of what we've been,
Though we transgressed He takes our slate
And wipes the surface clean.

His armour that we've girded on
Sits lightly on the frame,
The breastplate, the shield of faith
Which quench the darts of flame.

The helmet of salvation guards
The thoughts along the way,
Helping each pilgrim to withstand
The evil of the day.

Then we are more than conquerors
Against the devil's horde,
Not through our might, nor by our power,
But by the Spirit of the Lord.

John Frew

MEDITATION IN AN EMPTY CHURCH

When travelling, I oft go inside
A church in summer just to bide
And seek a time of quiet and cool
'Midst stonework architectural.

I view the pillars that uphold
The rafters where music has rolled,
From Christian voice and organ chord
In hymns that magnify the Lord.

How many Grooms have wed their Brides
Or little infants been baptised,
How many souls have knelt to pray
Whose breath has long since passed away?

Though rows of pews in silence stand
There's one that testifies a hand,
Had felt the strongest urge it should
Carve some initials in the wood.

Perhaps a soldier battle bound
Had sought a place on hallowed ground,
Entered in for fervent prayer
And signified that he'd been there?

Poetically Speaking

Angelic cherubs underpin
A plaque set in the wall within,
Whilst gargoyles on the wall without
Wait rainless by their waterspout.

And ranks of headstones signify
The folk beneath have now passed by,
Did they in life discard the leaven
And store some treasures up in heaven?

Many a Christian has avowed
There are no pockets in a shroud,
And poor man rich man, even King,
Must relinquish everything.

For flesh like grass will pass one day
As the flower head falls away,
What then are goods and chattels worth
To us reposing in the earth?

The Bible says we all must die
And that means you, yes, even I,
Seek the Lord while He may be found
If your desire be heaven bound.

WISE MEN LAY UP KNOWLEDGE

Lift up your heads you pilgrims
Trust in the Saviour's power,
And rest assured, He will return
Though no one knows the hour.

Keep looking for that blessed hope,
Your lamps well trimmed and bright,
When He returns He will arrive
As a thief comes in the night.

Hold fast through all adversities
And do not be deceived,
Our salvation is much nearer than
The day we first believed.

God shakes the world with earthquake
Wild tempest, flood and fire,
And weakens thrones and kingdoms
If He should so desire.

Have we not witnessed awesome scenes
Of devastating force,
The elements of our Sovereign Lord
On their catastrophic course?

The fool that says: "There is no God,"
Will receive no recompense,
Whereas the wise redeemed by Him
Are endued with common sense.

For such as read God's Holy Book
See much that is concealed,
A revelation to the questing mind
That His prophets have revealed.

THE LIGHT OF THE WORLD

Inside St Paul's Cathedral
A picture can be found,
By Holman Hunt, the artist
A painter well renowned.

Depicted is a wooden door
Forbidding and severe,
Hidden deep in ivy
Little daylight enters here.

Before it waits Christ Jesus
The Saviour of mankind,
Who, as he stands and gently knocks,
Has but one thought in mind.

In almost every human heart
Are tears, and hurt, and sorrow,
He knows He has the answer
For everyone's tomorrow.

His Grace, and Love, and Mercy,
Are boundless and quite free,
To all who humbly do repent
In true sincerity.

The single latch upon the door
Is only found within,
So why not open it my friend
And let the Saviour in?

THE DIVINE HEALER

"Master", the disciples asked,
for they wanted to know why,
"Who sinned, was it the blind man,
or his parents years gone by?"

"None of them", replied the Lord,
as they paused to take a rest,
"But in order that the work of God
through him be manifest".

For we must work the works of Him
who sent me whilst it's day;
The night will come when non can work
when the light has passed away."

Jesus spat upon the ground
to constitute some clay,
Then spread the paste upon the eyes
of the blind man where he lay.

"Now go and wash within the pool
of Siloam", said the Lord;
He did so, and, when he returned
his sight had been restored.

The Pharisees were sore displeased
at the work that had been done,
But could not see the miracle was
performed by God's own Son.

They questioned yet again the man:
"What did he do to you:
How did he open up your eyes
that you now see all things new?"

Said he: "Did you not listen?
from God my healer came,
He also is a prophet
though I do not know his name."

The Pharisees were furious,
and yet thought themselves devout,
They said: "You were born in utter sin",
and from the synagogue cast him out.

Then Jesus sought the man and said:
"Do you believe the Son of man?"
He answered: "And who is he sir?
I'd like to if I can."

The Lord replied: "You've seen him,
it is he that speaks to you,"
And the man bowed down and worshipped Him
for now at last he knew.

We praise you and we thank you Lord,
in humble genuflection,
For the assurance that you're always there
should we suffer man's rejection.

John Frew

LOST AND FOUND

I heard the tale of a little boy
Who got lost in London town,
He'd been shopping for his mother
When a swirling fog came down.

He stopped beneath a lamppost
In its pool of yellow light,
Sobbing uncontrollably
When he realised his plight.

A kindly Bobby happened by
As he patrolled his beat,
And he looked down at the little chap
Who had tearstains on his cheek.

"Lost your bearings have you lad,
And can't find your abode?
Well; it shouldn't be too hard to find
If you can name your street or road.

Is it near a railway station,
Some shops, or cinema?"
"I can't remember", sobbed the boy,
"But I hope it's not too far."

Then suddenly his eyes lit up
And he brightened visibly,
He recalled a place, which he knew well
That would provide the key.

"There's a big white cross nearby my home
and it stands inside the Square
if you could take me to it Sir,
I know my way from there."

THE ULTIMATE JOURNEY

When we die so shall we lie
Just as the tree that falls,
Too late to change or rearrange
Our ways when our Master calls.

The instant that a saint departs
In a higher place is he,
And happier than the richest man
On earth could ever be.

If men and women everywhere
Would but take time and think,
Only repentance and true faith
Can save them from the brink.

No purgatory awaits the soul
Or conversion in the ground,
The frame remains, the spirit goes,
But where will it be found?

In the glorious presence of the Lord
Or in torment and unrest?
Time waits for no man, seek Him now
And make known you request.

For the moment a believer dies
In heaven he will be,
That is the promise Jesus gave
To the thief upon the tree.

To the uttermost the Lord can save
A sinner from his fate,
But foolish would be any man
To leave it quite so late.

John Frew

FOR HE WILL SHUT THE HEAVENS AND THEY SHALL BE AS BRASS

We have heard the sabres rattling
And the rumbling talk of war,
Though there is nothing new in that
We've been down that road before.

They say the English love to fight
That it's something we do well,
Though we always have to pay the price
As our war memorials tell.

There was a time when the longbow,
The cutlass, sword and shield,
Were the arms that caused our enemies
To lay down theirs and yield.

And Lord Nelson gained the victory
Over the French and Spanish fleets,
Whilst Wellington's triumph at Waterloo
Brought rejoicing in our streets.

Then in two world wars we had just cause
To repel the German horde,
And such was the faith of our nation then
We fought in the strength of the Lord.

Those were the days when the chaplains prayed
And we acknowledged God's greatness and might,
The church prayed on its knees
And he honoured our pleas
And preceded us into the fight.

How does God rate us today,
Does He hear when we pray?
For as a nation we've sinned in His sight,
Governed by fools who have trampled His rules
And too proud to put matters right.

GETHSEMANE

Across the Kidron brook they went
Unsure what lay ahead,
Through a grove of gnarled old olive trees
Where Jesus stopped and said,
"Every one of you will fall away
This night because of me:
It is written, 'Strike the shepherd
And the flock of sheep will flee."

He then took Simon Peter
With the brothers James and John,
To a small outcrop of rocky ground
A few more paces on.
The Son of Man then urged the three,
"Let watchfulness abound."
Then in sorrow deep, and great distress
Fell prostrate on the ground.

He agonised in prayer, three times,
There in Gethsemane
"Abba Father, couldst thou not,
Remove this cup from me?"
Against His wish the disciples slept
On that holy piece of land
Then Jesus shook them saying,
"My betrayer is at hand."

Then came a crowd, with swords and clubs,
And the priests and scribes whose quest
Was to trap the one whom Judas kissed,
And make a false arrest.
When the Lamb of God was led away
No disciples were in sight,
And the blood of Christ would ever stain
Those silver coins that night.

GOLGOTHA

When across the Kidron valley they
Came to take Jesus away,
Our Lord to Judas said just this,
"wouldst thou betray me with a kiss?"

Jesus, the man who days before
They'd hailed as King on palm-strewn floor,
The Light who came the world to save
Now they clamoured for His early grave.

Scourged at the post in Pilate's yard
Punched in the face by Roman guard,
His Holy countenance contused,
And body marbled, striped and bruised.

This was the bitter cup that He
Visualised in Gethsemane,
A scene Isaiah once foresaw
Several hundred years before.

In purple robe and vicious crown
Of thorns, they brought our Saviour down
To suffer Pilate's jurisdiction,
As the crowd bayed for His crucifixion.

Said Pilate, unsure what to do,
"I'm giving your King back to you"
"He's not our King", the priests replied,
as they took him to be crucified.

How deep the grief, how great the loss,
How cruel those dark hours on the Cross
When Jesus, Prophet Priest and King,
For us surrendered everything.

NO GREATER LOVE

The grain of frankincense with wine
Which women offered at the time
To felons condemned to the tree
Was meant to ease their agony.
Christ spurned the drink that deadened pain
Intent that he should know the same
That mortal man was forced to bear
And He was destined to be there.

In the shadow of our Saviour's tree
Four Roman guards knelt callously
Gambling; their avaricious eyes
Set upon the greatest prize,
His cloak; with Rabbi's tasselled hem
One soul once touched her blood to stem.
This was our Lord, who only came
To cure the blind, the sick, and lame,
Casting out demons and pardoning sin
In those tormented deep within.

Great darkness caused the sun to fail,
Rent in twain was the Temple veil,
The way to God was opened then
His sacrifice had shown to men
No greater love would mankind see
'Neath God's celestial canopy.
From the cross there came the Saviour's cry
"The work is done, Tetelestai."

SIGNS OF THE TIMES

Have you heard some people say
So much is wrong with the world today?
Its wars and famine, fires and flood
And wanton spilling of human blood.

The innocence of youth reviled
Or murder of a little child
Nor even are the elderly
Looked upon respectfully.

Sometimes a thrust from a mugger's knife
Robs someone of their precious life
Or use of an illegal gun
Consigns a soul to oblivion.

There is a reason for all this
It's hate and lust and avarice,
Man's inhumanity to man
Take what you want, grab all you can.

And many too will not endure
God's doctrine that is sound and pure,
Their itching ears are more inclined
To teachings of another kind.

No politician, sage or king
Has yet come forth with anything
To guarantee eternal peace
And animosity to cease.

But God be praised, there's one who can
Our Saviour Lord, the Son of man
Let's pray they'll hear His constant plea,
"Forsake you sins, and follow me."

TOO MUCH SUN A DESERT MAKES, BUT WE GET TOO MUCH RAIN.

I part the curtains every morning
To view the kind of day that's dawning,
And confess I'm apt to gripe and grizzle
At the incessant damp and dreary drizzle.

The spacial dome high overhead
Is as grey as a roofer's sheet of lead,
I wish the sky was a different hue
Azure perhaps, or duck egg blue.

Sun seekers jet above the cloud
We squelch beneath our misty shroud;
Their sky is blue, the nimbus white,
We, waterlogged are deprived of light.

Some mobile homes now rise on floats
Which gets the caravaner's votes,
As they watch the flood go swirling by
Their homes and contents safe and dry.

I think of Noah and his Ark
He chose the oddest place to park,
Half way up Mt Ararat
What did Mrs Noah think of that?

Fortune smiles on those who have found
Their homes sit on higher ground,
Others deserve our commiseration
When they suffer the annual inundation.

But putting aside all sentiments,
Is God speaking to us through His elements?
That He harnesses Nature there's no doubt,
Could it be He is working His purpose out?

John Frew

THE ALPHA AND THE OMEGA

He is the one with eyes of fire
And hair as white as wool,
Who stands among the lampstands
And He, no man can fool.

His feet shine forth like burnished bronze
Refined as in a fire,
His voice like many waters sound
Above His robed attire.

With golden girdle round His breast,
And face bright as the sun,
He is the first, He is the last,
He is the Holy one.

The lamps He tends are churches,
Which He trims so that they might,
Shine forth amidst the darkness
Of a world that needs His light.

How does the church of Albion stand,
What thinks He of our role,
And the years lost to the canker worm,
Will He restore them whole?

Take not away our lampstand Lord
But trim it that we may,
Burn more brightly and repent
Of our Laodicean way.

Save us Lord both from ourselves
And the enemy within,
Our parched souls plead your righteous rain
For new life to begin.

THE PARISH CHURCH

Most people say it's nice to see
A church with spire or tower,
With moss and lichens everywhere
And clock chimes on the hour.

Those solid flint and dressed stone walls
Have stood the test of time,
A symbolic kind of gesture
That everything is fine.

When ringers pull their sallies
The bells respond and chime,
Urging us to 'Come to Church,
Give God some of your time'.

A million souls across the world
Would forfeit everything,
Just for the freedom we enjoy
To worship Christ the King.

We suffer no repression
And our country will stay free,
Providing we uphold the faith
And our Christianity.

THE SANDS OF TIME

It was written: "There is a tide in the life of men
Which taken at the flood,
Leads on to fortune, even fame,
But omitted ends in misery and shame."
Sage advice for optimistic youth
About to launch itself upon
A world that waits with eagerness
The entrepreneurs of inventiveness.
I wonder why we in the West
Were once supernally greatly blessed;
Our multifarious skills are no illusion,
Remember the Industrial Revolution?

Yet our Stonehenge leaning in stark relief
Like neglected, broken, rotting teeth
Can scarce compare with what the Egyptians did
When they built their Sphinx and the Pyramid.
And the Sumerians of ancient Babylonia
From whom the science of numbering comes
Bequeathed to the world a title
Which arithmetically we now call 'sums'.
Yet Ishmael's descendants have it seems
Missed out in the world's technological schemes,
But God did endow them with wealth untold
In vast fields of oil we call 'black gold'.

But permit me now to show you
Something of a revelation,
I discovered concealed within 'Ishmael'
The religion of his nation.
By removing the letters H and E
From the name of Abraham's son
The remaining letters when rearranged
Spell out the word, 'Islam'.
Then I read the scriptures where I see
Jesus warns of a great apostasy,
Which begs the question: "Does Almighty God
Plan using Islam as His rod?"

John Frew

HAVE FOUR HORSEMEN
BEEN OUT RIDING?

For centuries much speculation
About the Book of The Revelation
Has exercised the minds of men
As to what will happen, how, and when.
John wrote, 'Blessed are they who read
The prophetic word and pay heed,
And blessed are they who pause to hear
For the time in question is getting near'.
The White Horse was the first to go
Its rider crowned and bearing bow,
To fulfil his obligations
In allowing kings to create nations.

Then the rider on the Red Horse rode
And two massive world wars came,
'He was given a great sword',
There were many millions slain.
We hear his hoof beats even now
The earth is robbed of peace,
There are tribal wars to settle scores
The bloodshed does not cease.
Kalashnikov's around the world
Cough and spit their hate,
Child soldiers even carry them,
Some can scarcely tote the weight.

The Ordnance of war lies everywhere
When the Red Horse has passed by;
Land mines lie low, no one dares hoe,
Lest they be blown sky high.
The rider on the Black Horse too
Has been traversing the land,
Rationing food with the crossbeam
Of a balance in his hand.
And legion are the people dead
Who stared famine in the eye,
Or died from Aids and pestilence
When the Pale Horse galloped by.

ONWARD CHRISTIAN SOLDIERS

Christian soldiers still march on
Marching as to war,
Though fewer numbers march today
Than did in days of 'yore.
Well my mother was a Christian,
Indeed my father too,"
That may be so, the question is,
"What does Jesus mean to you?"
God gave man rules in black and white
Sufficient for each day,
Some choose to misinterpret them
In uncertain shades of grey.

If the Salt should lose its savour
And embrace the devil's mirth,
What hope then for our children
And Christ's Church militant in earth?
Besides, when man is out of step with God
And the aegis of His power,
He condemns himself to walk alone
Come the deeply trouble hour.
Surely then our fight must be
In these dangerous days and hours,
Engaged not just with flesh and blood,
But dark principalities and powers.

I think of Troy and the wooden horse
With the enemy hid within,
And am persuaded that Britannia's trial
Must one day soon begin.
Like Shadrack, Meshach, and Abed'nego,
Who made God their sole desire,
We will need the Lord to walk with us
Should we traverse through the fire.
We were once renowned throughout the world
As, "The people of The Book",
Awake Britannia lest we become,
"The Land that God forsook".

CHERITON

Cheriton's existence, it appears
Numbers some eight hundred years,
Known thirty-six monarchs, both king and queen
And progressed from horsepower to gasoline.
It saw Roundhead and Royalist fight
And the Cavaliers trounced and put to flight.
The Black Death too brought deep decline
In thirteen hundred and forty-nine.
St. Michaels Church still stands four square
With Cranmer's Book of Common Prayer,
The faithful know today as then,
How well both serve the souls of men.
On the monument by the village green
Cut in stone, names can be seen
Of men who all fought valiantly
To keep our cherished Island free.
Before the arrival of amps and ohms
Oil lamps and candles lit our homes,
And kitchen kettles whistled hard
When fuelled by logs from Freeman's Yard.
It was a thriving business then
Giving work to countless village men.

The blacksmith left and went afar,
For who needs shoes for the motor car?
Two pub's have closed and landlords gone,
But the 'Flower Pots Inn' is brewing strong.
The village structure stays much the same
Between North End and Lamborough Lane.
But the old country folk have disappeared
Their homes enlarged or re-engineered.
And gone the men with their rural skill
To rest in the churchyard on the hill.
Yet in spite of all the changes seen
And of this or that which might have been,
The Itchen river runs bright and clear
Beneath nine bridges all the year.
Birds abound upon the wing
And the cuckoo stops by in the spring.
Our village becomes a quiet retreat
When the outside world turns on the heat,
And hopefully any change we make
Will not just be for change's sake.

WHERE WENT THE GENTLE YEARS?

Those former days of gentler ways
Can still be brought to mind,
When adolescent attitudes
Were of a different kind.
Compared with what we see today
Good manners were the norm,
Teachers were respected and
School children would conform.

Ludo, draughts, and snakes and ladders
Were thought to be terrific,
With Snap, and Chess and Dominoes
If you would have me more specific.
And in playgrounds you would see
Coloured whipping tops awhirl,
Marbles and fag cards for the boys
And skipping rope for girl.

There was an air of innocence
In youngsters of that day,
They could walk to school in safety
And to their local park to play.
Remembered too the summers when
Teenaged girls donned Sunday best,
And in cotton frocks and flower trimmed hats
Went to Church with all the rest.

ASPIRATIONS

Every living soul it seems
Nurtures longings, hopes, or dreams,
A few with genius luck or flair
Make the grade to millionaire.
Or don the cap and gown attire
To study 'neath the dreaming spire,
Striving to gain some high degree
From science to philosophy.

Yet others not so well endowed
Make up by far the larger crowd,
Whose industry and enterprise
Helps smooth the running of our lives.

Honest toil no one should shirk,
Man needs to eat so he must work,
But surprisingly a few elite
Merely live that they might eat.
Though rich as Croesus some may be,
Most would empathically agree,
There is no gain in untold wealth
Without the priceless gift of health.

John Frew

AUTUMN'S END

Bare stood the trees
Dispossessed of their leaves,
And a mist hovered over the stream;
While a heron stood by
With a glint in his eye,
Awaiting a fingerling's gleam.

Then a silvery trill
Left a robin's bill,
As the sky gathered clouds in the dusk;
And two sparrows worked late
To clear from a plate,
The very last seed from the husk.

When the clock in the tower
Of the church struck the hour,
An owl ghosted by on patrol;
Perhaps later tonight
He will hoot with delight,
Should he dine on a mouse or a vole.

Came the sounds of a hymn
From the organ within,
Through the stained glass windows light shone;
And illumined the night
With the bright coloured light,
Of the Saints, Matthew, Mark, Luke, and John.

ROOTS

I sat beneath an ancient yew
With God's acre in full view,
Content to know when I've run life's race
Yonder lies my resting place.
Thankful too that I never did
Expire upon some rocky ridge
In India, or Baluchistan
Or Burma and the Arakan:
Not to mention Africa
Where later during peaceful years
Sojourned for almost eighteen years.

The nomadic life when young is fine,
But as we age there comes a time
Long after the fire and zest of youth,
To admit there is a grain of truth
That over zealous career pursuits
Prevents us putting down some roots.
Rejecting too that sly old bluff
That of money we'll not have enough.

This Hampshire village where I live
Always had a lot to give,
And my friendly cottage through the years
Witnessed our laughter, love and tears.
Such cherished memories correspond
With its brick and flint to form a bond.
Then there's the grave that verifies
The place where my own darling lies.
How does a poet first begin
To pen his thoughts and reasoning?
Well, I was seated beneath an ancient yew
With God's acre in full view...

Printed in the United Kingdom
by Lightning Source UK Ltd.
107558UKS00001B/175-270